Under the Sea

by Ruth Owen

Editorial consultant: Mitch Cronick

ticktock

CONTENTS

Words in **bold** are explained in the glossary.

Peek at the coral reef

There is a lot to see
on a **coral reef**.

Diver

Coral

Fish

5

Starfish

The starfish has five legs.

Its mouth is under here.

Blue starfish

Orange starfish

Clownfish

Clownfish live on coral reefs.

They have white and orange stripes.

Clownfish

This is an animal
called a sea sponge.

10

Sea sponges

Look at the octopus

The octopus has eight legs.

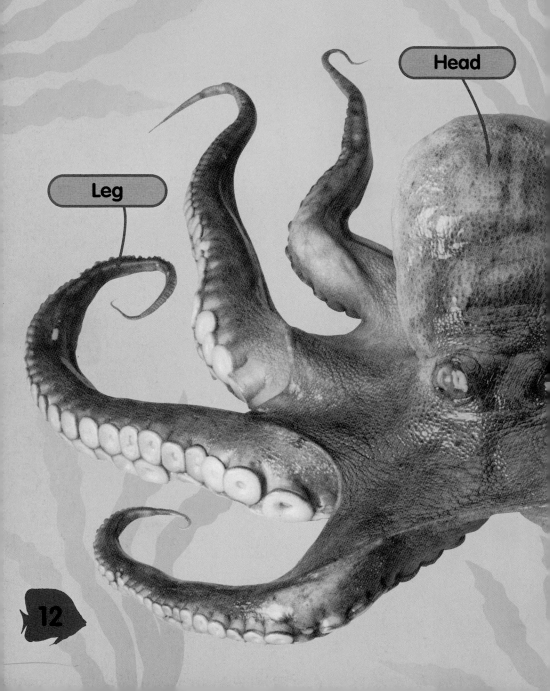

Head

Leg

It gets red when it's angry!

Look at the lobster

It has two big **claws**.

Claws

The lobster has eight legs.

Look at the crab

The crab has a hard **shell**.

Red crab

Claw

What is a seahorse?

A seahorse is a kind of fish.

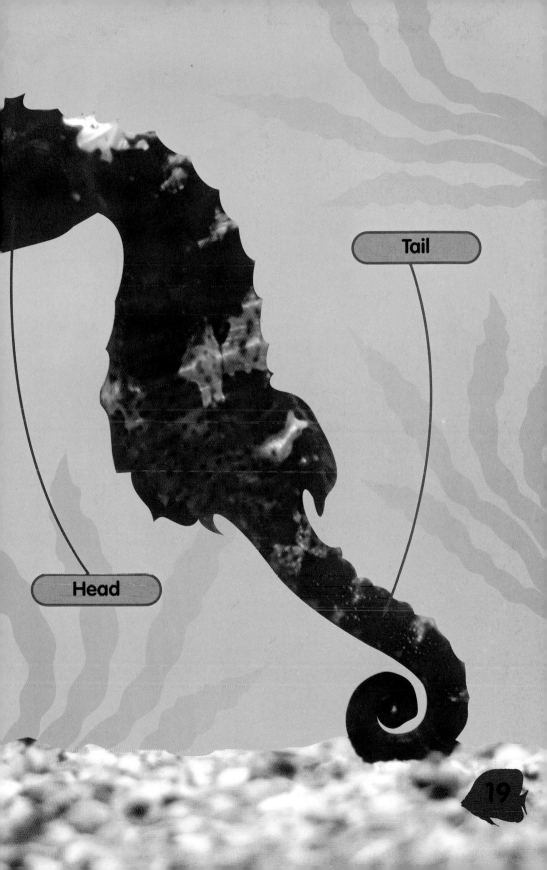

Tail

Head

The hungry turtle

The turtle eats fish, crabs and lobsters.

Shell

Legs

Glossary

claw

A body part with two pointy sections.
A claw is used to grab things.

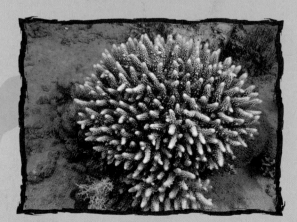

coral

A little sea animal that
lives in a big group.

coral reef

An underwater place made from the hard, dead bodies of corals. The reef looks as if it is made from rock.

shell

The hard outside part of an animal's body.

Index

Publisher: Melissa Fairley
Studio Manager: Sara Greasley
Editor: Emma Dods
Designer: Trudi Webb
Production Controller: Ed Green
Production Manager: Suzy Kelly

ISBN: 978 1 84898 112 6